A Poetic J...

For
Healing, Hope, and Purpose

A Poetic Walk of Faith

For
Healing, Hope, and Purpose

Alesia W. Green

Writers Café Publishing Co.
Charlotte, NC.

Library of Congress Control Number: 2006903128

First published by AuthorHouse
4/27/2006
Bloomington, IN

First Revision 5/16/2008
Second Revision 2/1/2009
by
Writers Café Publishing
Charlotte, NC

Printed in the United States of America
Charlotte, NC

CONTENTS

<u>Dedication</u>

This book is dedicated to all women worldwide.

As a single mother of three I have experienced the challenges of carrying a heavy load full of responsibilities and stress. I found myself in a vicious cycle of running from place to place trying to fulfill an endless "to do list". I struggled and juggled until I completely burned out of energy. Mentally and physically broken, I cried out to the LORD to help me. My cry was hot with fury because I was mad at the world. I asked God, "What am I supposed to do"! Why am I here? What's the point?"

God heard my cry and He showed up! He showed up to let me know that He is real! I was overjoyed and amazed! But then out of nowhere I felt a slight since of fear and embarrassment about some things that I had done in the past. All of those bad things flashed through my mind in a matter of seconds. Then out of nowhere, I felt a strong force moving me to confess all of those sins and to plea to Him for forgiveness. I knew that He had forgiven me when I felt an immense sense of relief. It was as if a load of heavy bricks were lifted off of my shoulders. Tears of joy flowed down my face replacing the overwhelming amount of painful tears of the past. It was on that day that I surrendered my life to God by asking him to direct my steps so that I will do his will and not my own. I became a born again Christian washed clean of all of my past sins and transgressions through the blood of the Lamb, Jesus Christ.

Jesus died on the cross to save me and you (Psalm 116:3&6) He has blessed us with the opportunity to live with him on a renewed earth for eternity. Yes, Jesus died so that we may have eternal life! (John 3:16). Now that's what you can call true love!

On a daily basis I strive to walk close as possible in the footsteps of Jesus with hopes to be found worthy to enter the Kingdom of God (Colossians 1:10-14). In the Kingdom of God there will be no more tears, no more death, or mourning, or crying, or pain (Revelation 21:3 & 4).

Each of us has a specific purpose in life which God has predestine for us. However there is one purpose that all Christian share. Once we have healed from our past and have grown in our faith we must share our testimony with those who are going through what we have already gone through. We must help them find salvation. Encourage them so that they may stay strong and not be tempted to fall back into their old ways. We must tell others that Jesus is the only true solution to every problem in life and there is no problem that God cannot fix. Encourage them to establish a strong personal relationship with God. Let them know that God and Jesus are the best friends that any of us could ever have. In times of trouble we will be comforted by The Holy Spirit sent to us by God Himself. God is always with us and watching over us. So there you have it. Now we know what true love, peace, and security is. It is God!

*This volume of poetry is sectioned into potential stages of a journey. Each journey will vary depending upon each individual's unique set of life circumstances. For example, one person may be able to identify with only one poem in the "Please Heal Me Lord..." discussion and poems. However, another may identify with two or more. None-the-less, each individual should be able to track how far she has come on her journey as she advances from one section to the next. I pray that no one will be stuck in the "**Please Help Me Lord!!!**" section. This is the hardest level to get through, but you have the strength and the power to make it out of there. Hold on to Jesus. He is your helper.*

Below I have listed several scriptures to support the subtitle of this book which is "<u>For Healing, Hope, and Purpose</u>".

> *Do not be conformed any longer to the pattern of this world, but be transformed by the renewing of your mind.*
> *(Romans 12:2)*

> *For we are God's workmanship, created in Christ Jesus to do good works, which God has prepared in advance for us to do.*
> *(Ephesians 2:10)*

Praise be to God and Father of our Lord Jesus Christ, the Father of compassion and the God of all comfort, who comforts us in all our troubles, so that we can comfort those in any trouble with the comfort we ourselves have received from God.
(2Corinthians 1:3-4)

I will instruct you and teach you in the way you should go; I will counsel you and watch over you.
(Psalm 32:8).

Acknowledgements

All thanks, glory, and praise go to God for the children that He has blessed me with. For them, I am motivated to carry on while God's grace allows me to carry on. I also thank God for my mother and father who have been there for me in times of trouble. Thanks also go to Pastor Emmitt Cornelius for reviewing the original version of this work for scriptural accuracy.

I pray for God to continue to stretch out his mighty arm with blessings of safety, security, peace, and happiness for all of His children worldwide.

Enclosed Is Your Invitation To Salvation...

(Please RSVP!!!)

Invitation to Salvation (RSVP)

Luke 21:10 & 11
Then he said to them: "Nation will rise against nation, and kingdom against kingdom. There will be great earthquakes, famines, and pestilences in various places, and fearful events and great signs from heaven."

Matthew 24:42
Therefore keep watch, because you do not know on what day your Lord will come.

Look at the signs around us. Evidence is becoming stronger that we are near the end of this age. Don't take for granted that you will be here tomorrow. Don't risk departing from this world without accepting Jesus Christ as Lord and Savior. Now more than ever is the time to begin getting your life in order. God is making it very clear that it is time to take a stand and choose which side you are on-- good or evil. There is no more straddling the fence or being lukewarm. You must decide because Jesus is coming back!

It's Sunday morning.
Service is almost over,
But before it comes to an end,
The Pastor searches the entire crowd over.

Looking for a raised hand,
Symbolizing a touched heart,
Feeling the need to get Christ in their life,
But kind of shy about how to start.

It's altar call again,
Another invitation to salvation to extend.
Come stake your claim to eternity.
Our Lord and Savior Jesus Christ is where all things begin and end.

Are you going to let another week go by
Without responding my friend?
Take a few moments to ponder over your decision.

In the meantime,
Let me bring a few biblical facts to your attention.

Time is running out!!
You can see evidence in the news and on TV.
Fearful events and a demoralized society
Snuck up on this world of people,
Rushing around full of anxiety.

Devastating earthquakes,
Hurricane Katrina, cyclones, and tsunamis.
Wars and rumors of wars,
Some of which we are still asking, "Why are we fighting?"

Terrorist attacks, famine, pestilence,
Stolen identities and cloning.
Homosexuality is accepted as normal.
This is an abomination to God!
Remember that is why he destroyed Sodom and Gomorrah!

These are a few end time events of kingdoms and nations.
Now let's see what the Bible says about human relations.

People will not be lovers of God;
Instead, they will be lovers of themselves,
Lovers of money,
Brutal and abusive,
Living life so unholy!

They will be boastful, arrogant, and full of pride,
Without love or an ounce of self -control dwelling inside.
Giving in to all ill and fleshly desires
With no time to even realize how close their soul is to fire.

People will be unforgiving and slanderous,
Full of selfish greed and corrupt.
Striving for riches that are meaningless
Because when the soul is taken away,
The body returns to dust.

The young will be errant,
Disrespecting their elders and disobedient to parents,
Wise way beyond their ages,
Sinfully weak…working for deadly wages.

These are things the Bible warns about.
It says when you see these things occurring,
"Be alert!" and "Keep watch!"
For Jesus will be coming soon,
And he will come like a thief in the night!!

WILL YOU BE READY?
PLEASE (RSVP)

Please Heal Me Lord...

Forbidden Love

Song of Songs 2:7
Do not arouse or awaken love until it so desires.

Psalm 130:5
I wait for the LORD, my soul waits, and in his word I put my hope.

It seems that there are no good men left on this earth. None-the-less, much effort is put into searching for one. Eagerness to put faith and trust into a man continually meets with disappointment. Put an end to this relentless search. Relax and ask God to send the person that he knows will be right for you and your children. Then be patient, trust Him, and wait.

Why do good women love men that are so hard to reach?
Living in their presence but never with them completely:

So desirable it seems...
Like the Forbidden Tree,
And Adam and Eve,
While in the Garden of Eden.

Remember...
The day that they ate of that tree they surely did die.

~~~~~~

This happens to good women more than justified:
Love so intense...
Love thought meant to be...
Yet repeatedly denied.

Love stolen:
By a mistress named Cocaine.

A woman down the way seducing her man:
Creeping to see him,
Ringing his cell phone every chance that she can.

Love of the charming:
He is big on deception and gamin'.
Eventually his actions reveal an extreme lack of home training.

Love for a hardened heart:
Deep inside he is really a good man,
But his heart has been broken so many times before.
He has vowed to never love again.

~~~~~~

Each event takes her backwards and drags her down.
Once again, she is drained and tired.
Her heart is fragmented, swollen and hollow.

Each love was too far to reach even though she kept trying.
Reaching, reaching…to grab a hand.
But with each attempt fell another man.

When she calls on the LORD,
He hears her cry and He comes running.
He has been watching…
And He is happy that she finally decided to consult Him,
And because He loves her, He issues a warning:

When red flags go up,
Put your heart on lock down!
Only God can redeem souls,
That Satan has thrown awry.

Be warned: Do not eat until God's work is complete!
Just pray for their souls with heartfelt cries.

For if you do not wait...
The day that you eat of them your heart will surely die.

~~~~~~

A wise woman will ask...
Please LORD,
Take this pain away.
Please make my heart whole again.
You know that I am a good woman.
I just want a good man.

If it's your will,
Please reveal to me **your** choice of a man.
In the meantime, show me how to be happy while single.
Please show me how to trust **your** plan.

Motherless Child

Psalms 27:10
Though my father and mother forsake me, the LORD will receive me.

Psalm 127:3
Sons are a heritage from the LORD, children a reward from him.

Many children today are victims of parental neglect. There are also many adults with emotional scars from childhood neglect. The absence of a father is tragic in itself, but the absence of a good maternal figure proves to be even more devastating to a child. Traditionally, mothers have provided the nurturing which molds children into mentally and emotionally healthy adults. Sadly, the demoralization of society and drug addiction has produced many mothers who lack natural maternal instincts. Instead, there is a selfish, "It's all about me" attitude. Children are no longer a top priority. Satan has lured both mothers and fathers away from their God- given responsibilities. This crisis seems to get worse with each generation. If you are or have been a victim of parental neglect, let that cycle end with you. **Beware of neglecting your children. God is watching, and children are very special to Him!!!** Mothers, fathers, and children should get to know about our Lord and Savior Jesus Christ. Let Him heal your scars and forgive your sins. Your family can have a new life in Jesus Christ.

Confusion, sadness, madness, and fear--
I am looking for mother,
But I can't find her anywhere.

~~~~~~

Never before seen so many raised without her.
Brought in the world neglected all the while.
How do they learn, how do they grow?

Where is your mother child?

22

What a blow to the community, the city, the world.
The un-nurtured child, whether it be a boy or a girl
Makes for a dangerous society already gone wild.
No sense of family for this motherless child.
What happened to God's master plan,
For man and woman to unite fruitfully,
To bear and raise children
Honestly, respectfully, and lovingly?

Where is your mother child?

~~~~~~

She's not home and it's two hours past twelve.
Mom's out clubbing with her friend.
He is fresh out of jail.
She is flirting and drinking...
I wish she would forget-me-not,
But she wants to show the world that she is still really hot.

She has been told by many people that she needs to be home,
Cleaning up and cooking some meals.
But she says, "No, not me baby,
That doesn't fit my bill."
Why doesn't she ask,
"Is homework done?"
"Are chores complete?"
I guess it's not her concern while she is out running the streets.

Hey, come look who is walking way down there.
She is hot, sassy, sexy, and trashy.

There's my mother!
Ain't that what you asked me?

Without a care in the world,
She forgot her little boy and little girl.
That's why I feel like a motherless child,
Trying to figure out this cold, cold world.

~~~~~~

Oh yeah, I see your mother.
We will have to pray for her dear.

But you ask God
To heal your confusion,
Sadness, madness, and fear.

Our heavenly Father is always home.
He has plenty of love to give.
Dear child, you will never be alone.

A Secret Place

Psalms 91:1
He who dwells in the shelter of the Most High will rest in the shadow of the Almighty.

Jeremiah 33:6
I will heal my people and will let them enjoy abundant peace and security.

Unfortunately, some very tragic events have occurred in the lives of many people, both young and old. Some victims carry tragedy with them daily in their minds, thereby becoming captives of a mental prison. Some victims attempt to console their pain by seeking comfort in other forms of misconduct. However, confronting tragedy is the only true source of healing. Healing cannot work its spirit cleansing therapy on issues which are swept away and kept under rugs. Remove guilt and shame by eliminating the need to hide your unfortunate experiences from the world. Ask God for deliverance from your mental prison. After healing is complete and guilt and shame are conquered, reach out to help other victims. Share with others how being washed in the blood of the Lamb has allowed you to exchange guilt and shame for renewed innocence and honor.

My heart and my mind are locked in a secret place.
Memories and hurt from the past
I try to erase.

They keep trying to escape,
To show off in my words and actions,
To make people look at me strangely;
Hurt and pain breaks away to nourish its own satisfaction.

Nobody ever told me that it wasn't my fault.
Nobody ever told me that I should not be ashamed.
Nobody ever told me to stop feeling dirty.
Nobody ever told me to stop taking the blame.

As I stand in this building many stories high,
I stare out of a window.
A tear falls from my eye.

How I wish I could walk across this crisp blue sky.
I would skip from cloud to cloud,
With visions of peace in my mind.

Oh how light I would feel.
My heart and mind would begin to heal.
In a new secret place,
Where everything is surreal.

~~~~~~

I enter this new secret place.
And the LORD is waiting,
To my surprise!
I am surrounded by His grace.
Glory glistens from His eyes.

He told me that it wasn't my fault.
He told me not to be ashamed.
He told me to stop feeling dirty.
He told me to stop taking the blame.

He said come find peace with me my child.
His arms were cradled as for a baby.
He told me to let hurt and pain go,
So that I…May become…A brand new lady.

Please Lord...Forgive Your Child

Proverbs 28:13
He who conceals his sins does not prosper, but whoever confesses and renounces them find mercy.

Romans 6:21
What benefit did you reap at that time from the things that you are now ashamed of? Those things result in death!

Even Christians sometimes stumble and fall because we are still imperfect humans. However, we find that we fall less and less as we mature in our faith. If ever we find ourselves in a fallen state, we must confess with our mouth, repent, and petition God for forgiveness. If we are sincere, our kind and merciful heavenly Father will gladly receive us back into His grace with open arms. He will lift us back up high!

Please forgive me LORD.
For I have done wrong.
Knowingly, but not wantingly.
Never-the-less I have done wrong.

I can't take it back.
It's over now.
I should have been stronger, but I wasn't,
So now I cry.

Please LORD...forgive your child.

Passions of the heart,
Desires of the flesh
Prevent us from being our very best.

We beg for strength in times of temptation,
But when it looks and feels good, we forget our Godly relations.
What a mess we have now because we relinquished our protection.
Now we face the consequences of our challenged imperfections.

Please LORD…forgive your child.
For I have done wrong,
But I do not want to die.

Help me cope with situations that I created.
I pray that none are deathly related.

I must move on and continue to live.
This is a gift that you so graciously give.

Please LORD…forgive your child.
Lift me up and let me fly!

Please Help Me Lord!!!

Thug on the Prowl

Proverbs 26:24 & 25
A malicious man disguises himself with his lips,
but in his heart he harbors deceit.
Though his speech is charming, do not believe him, for seven abominations
fill his heart.

Proverbs 14:1
The wise woman builds her house, but with her own hands the foolish one
tear hers down.

We know who these people are. We have met them many times before. We may have even taken one in. This person will use a woman until she cannot be used anymore. He will move on when she does not give anymore. He will move on when she tells him that he needs to grow up and be responsible. However, he will stay if the woman gives in and does not stand her ground. With this type of person, we must face the fact that responsibility is not on his agenda. Maybe someday his agenda will change, but waiting to find out may not prove to be wise. Do not allow anyone to waste your time and disrupt your relationship with your children. You do not need a man to help you to do badly when you can do better without him. Trust in the LORD. He will help you all the way.

Be on the watch!
There's a thug on the prowl!
Plotting on the next single mother he finds.

Looking for a place to stay-
Rent free-
No bills to pay.

He'll charm his way in,
He will make you his fan.
Watch how he slowly executes his plan.
But don't let him get that far.
When you see him coming...

Turn around,
Do a 180!
I know his look is good,
But it's also kind of shady.

If you give this guy a minute,
He will take from you what seems to be a lifetime.
He will borrow your money-
Control your house-
Drive your car-
He will act as if he worked hard,
As if he purchased them all.

I tell you, beware of thugs on the prowl.
I really want you to understand that...

If you let him in,
He will move...right in.

I am trying to say this as clear as I can.
Just because he lives with you,
Does not make him your man!

Dancing With Wolves

2Corinthians 6:14
Do not be yoked together with unbelievers.
For what do righteousness and wickedness have in common? Or what
fellowship can light have with darkness.

1John 4:2 & 3
This is how you can recognize the Spirit of God: Every spirit that
acknowledges that Jesus Christ has come in the flesh is from God, but every
spirit that does not acknowledge Jesus is not from God.

Stop, red light! Think twice before you choose to entertain yourself outside of the body of Christ. Remember that worldly people operate according to an entirely different set of rules than Christians. Sometimes the world seems to be a place where there are no rules at all-- a place where any and everything goes. This becomes painfully vivid after a Christian has spent some time playing out there. Do not play on the playing field of those unevenly yoked with you. Wait for someone who adheres to the same set of beliefs that you do. This warning is for Christian males and females. Wolves come in both genders, and they all wear sheep's clothing very well.

Wolves in disguise:
They come in sheep's clothing,
Twisting, pulling, tugging, and coaxing.

Manipulating what they want you to do
Like a puppet on strings.
But to benefit who?

Intellectually playing on your mind,
Massaging your heart,
Smile looking so kind.
They are so deceiving with eyes so believing.

34

What a talent,
An art,
How did this slow dance start?

Dancing with wolves on a slow mystical song,
Your mind becomes a blur;
Something feels very wrong.

Now you're feeling ill and cheated because he has gone on his way.
You're not sure that you can face another day.
Who can you love, who do you date, who can you marry?
You do not want to hate…

You're suffering from negative vibes.
Because someone you thought was special perpetuated lies.
But it was you, who ignored that little voice,
And God's spirit inside.

A voice warning you to beware.
To get away from it all.
Begging, please stop the music!
Don't dance anymore!

Remember that dancing with wolves is a dangerous game.
They come in sheep's clothing, all wanting the same.

Rare Gem

Proverbs 20:15
Gold there is, and rubies in abundance, but lips that speak knowledge are a
rare jewel.

Proverbs 31:10
A wife of noble character who can find?
She is worth far more than rubies.

Never let anyone devalue you or underestimate you. You deserve to be treated with respect. If you are treating a man like a king, he should be treating you like a queen. Do not try to justify "give and take" scales that are out of balance. Stop telling a man what he should already know. Stop trying to convince him that you deserve better. A precious stone, a rare gem, is a treasure to be cherished. Ask God to send a man who will respect and cherish you without being told by you to do so.

He does not know what he has in a woman like you.
And if he doesn't know by now,
Don't tell him.

The evidence should be clear to his eyes.
You are such a prize.
All of his friends and family recognize.
But if he doesn't know by now,
Don't tell him.

You are a rare gem by his side.
There is nothing for you to ever hide.
You are faithful, true, and loyal too.
But if he doesn't know by now,
Don't tell him.

A precious diamond he throws away.
You have shown him more than words could ever say.
But if he doesn't know by now,
Don't tell him.

There will come a day when he will realize;
It will be so very clear before his eyes.

And he will know,
But you won't have to tell him
Because you will be the sparkle in another man's eyes.

This Time Ask God

Proverbs 13:20
He who walks with the wise grows wise,
but a companion of fools suffers harm.

Proverbs 26:12
Do you see a man wise in his own eyes?
There is more hope for a fool than for him.

Now let's get real ladies! How can we keep helping somebody if we cannot even help ourselves? We have all done it! We have enabled others to continue with destructive patterns and lifestyles which adversely affect themselves and everyone around them. Sometimes we label our own actions as showing love, having a heart, or having compassion for another. Well, sometimes those beautiful emotions and actions cripple those behaving foolishly. Sometimes we just need to back up or cut them off so that they will learn to stand up and face the consequences of their actions. Stop making it easy on them and hard on yourself. Send them to Jesus. There is no problem or problem person in life that is too difficult for God to handle.

If someone needs you
Who you have helped many times before,

If that someone constantly calls on you
Because he somehow thinks that his mess
Is always your chore.

~~~~~~

If this time, you are sitting and thinking:
What is going on?
I can't even help myself because I'm not feeling so strong.

38

But here he comes again!
What are you supposed to do?
How do you say "no" to a friend?

~~~~~~

You need to tell him:
This time, ask God,

You know that I will pray for you.

Tell him:
This time, ask God.
You have to face up to the things that you do.

Be honest:
Tell him that you can't take anymore
Because too much has happened.
Remind him that you have never failed him before.

Be honest:
Tell him that your well has run dry and all of your energy is gone.
And even though you want to help him, you cannot be his superstar.

**You need to tell him:
This time, ask God!**

A Tempting Situation

Matthews 26:41
"Watch and pray so that you will not fall into temptation. The spirit is willing, but the body is weak."

James 1:15
When tempted, no one should say, "God is tempting me." For God cannot be tempted by evil, nor does he tempt anyone; but each one is tempted when by his own evil desire, he is dragged away and enticed. Then, after desire has conceived, it gives birth to sin.

We will all face various forms of temptation in our Christian walk. Satan is always going to be out to get us. He will try to tempt us by playing on the weaknesses of our past. We cannot give him satisfaction by testing ourselves. We have to pray for strength in times of temptation, but we must also walk away at the same time. We cannot pray for strength in one breath, but then allow room for enticement in the next. Such a situation will most likely cause us to fall.

A tempting situation stirred up a battle inside of me.
Right versus wrong,
Do I carry on?
I need to get away from this situation that is trying me.

A tempting situation made my spirit low.
But I didn't have to fall.
I could have walked away.
I should have been stronger.

I thought about it for too long.
I tuned out God's spirit which guides me.

A tempting situation,
I relaxed and let it entice me.

Now a million tears I cry,
Begging Lord please help me.
But as I pick up His word,
I feel my spirit rise as He steps back inside me.

~~~~~~

This is a lesson to learn:
None of us has to fall.
With Jesus Christ, victory is in us all.

And we must always remember:
A tempting situation is merely a test of our integrity and dedication.

REJOICE IN THE POWER
TO OVERCOME!

Thorns in My Flesh

2 Corinthians 12:7
To keep me from becoming conceited because of these surpassingly great revelations, there was given me a thorn in my flesh, a messenger of Satan, to torment me. Three times I pleaded with the Lord to take it away from me. But he said,"My grace is sufficient for you, for my power is made perfect in weakness. Therefore I will boast all the more gladly about my weakness, so that Christ power shall rest on me.

Psalm 119:50 & 51
My comfort in my suffering is this:
Your promise preserves my life. The arrogant mock me without restraint, but I do not turn from your law.

How irritating are those thorns in our flesh! Most of the time, thorns are people who mock our faithfulness to God. Some do not believe that holiness and righteousness are necessary; others simply do not care. They do not understand what it means to walk by faith and not by sight. To them, waiting on the Lord and being obedient to Him is incomprehensible. We must thank our Lord for helping us when we are around these people. If it were not for His grace surrounding us, these people could easily ignite fire in our soul. We have to keep believing that God fulfills every promise that He makes. We must always walk by faith and not by sight.

What grief I had in my bones.
Thorns in my flesh walked triumphantly bold.

Coming in my presence to take from me,
Showing no appreciation for my Christ-like deeds.

Walking away with my kindness in the gift I gave away.
So I thought to myself...
Well, maybe "thank you" will come tomorrow.

But, it didn't…
Because tomorrow is now today.

~~~~~~

I went to my Father,
I asked Him to please take the grief away.

Then He said:

What are you doing sitting idle,
Allowing foolish thoughts to hunt you like prey?

Why are you worried about these people,
About what they do or what they say?

You are supposed to be busy doing my work,
While I am busy making your way.

Do not fret over them who strut proudly
Because their glory could very well last just for a day.

After all:
I am the One who allows them to have a rope to climb;
However, in the midst of the climb I can also take it away!

~~~~~~

That is when I rushed back to work,
And when I was done, I was okay!

Looks like being busy with my Father's work,
Is part of how He makes my day!

<u>All This Rushing & Stressing! But For What??</u>

Matthew 6:34
Therefore do not worry about tomorrow, for tomorrow will worry about itself. Each day has enough trouble of its own.

1Timothy 6:17
Command those who are rich in this present world not to be arrogant nor to put their hope in wealth, which is so uncertain, but to put their hope in God, who richly provides us with everything for our enjoyment.

We must calm down and slow down so that we may endure to the end of this age. We must trust that God will provide all of our needs according to His perfect timing. We cannot allow the time clocks, schedules, and deadlines of this world to send us into a mental break down. We cannot live life focused on material things of this world. If materialism, debt, or status seeking have become a beast and burden in your life, pray to God to release you from bondage. Ask Him to show you a better way of living abundantly that will not lead to insanity.

We are a manic depressed,
Bipolar nation.
Perplexed over the downfall of human creation.

People all stressed out,
Racing from here to there,
So caught up in themselves,
That they cannot even see,
That they-
Are not-
Really going anywhere.

Living paycheck to paycheck,
Robbing Peter to pay Paul,
Afraid each day that they will lose it all.

44

Striving for worldly gain,
Bill collectors driving them insane,
Attempts to juggle it all cause acute mental pain.

Having to medicate
To function and operate,
At a sub-par level…

Distress is embroidered in the face,
As it becomes more and more complex,
To survive this human race.

But even with medication, it's all too much to handle.
Without the Holy Cross,
Our hearts and minds are in shambles.

Without Jesus Christ,
Many end up
Strapped down,
Residing behind doors
That are made without handles.

~~~~~~

So keep your focus on Christ!
Don't you dare blink an eye!
He made the ultimate sacrifice.
He suffered and paid the price for our iniquities and sins.

Therefore;
Through Him,
All things are sound.
No matter what things may look or feel like right now.
And with our God's pure love and beautiful grace,
All disorder in our lives will be put perfectly in place.

Whose Child Is This?

Genesis 18:20 & 21
Then the LORD said, "The outcry against Sodom and Gomorrah is so great and their sins so grievous that I will go down and see if what they have done is as bad as the outcry that has reached me

Romans 13:13 & 14
Let us behave decently, as in the daytime, not in orgies and drunkedness, not in sexual immorality and debauchery, not in dissension and jealousy.

We have witnessed an extreme change in the lifestyles of children worldwide. This generation of children is often referred to as the "lost generation." They are caught up in every form of ungodliness. Many parents are trying hard to protect their young from the ways of the world, but Satan is so cunning. He slowly infiltrates desires of the flesh into the ears, eyes, and minds of children. He devours children with every form of entertainment and technology. He attracts and fascinates their minds with every unmentionable sexual desire through songs and music videos. He instills an appetite for violence through video games and movies. Notice how many regular TV network channels air sitcoms that condone the gay lifestyle. The internet is a magnet for child molesters and producers of child pornography. Cell phones keep the young busy texting instead of engaging in constructive works. CD players secretly pump vulgar music in their ears. Fighting against all of these things is more than any parent can do on their own. Again, only God can save the souls of those led astray by Satan. Give the child to Jesus in prayer.

My child has bumped **HIS** head!
My child has lost **HER** mind!

The one I gave birth to,
The one I nurtured and protected.
And even though I was not perfect,
This child received my very best.

46

But regardless of what I have done,
No matter how hard I have tried,
Wickedness has whisked my child away.
This child, I can no longer identify.

~~~~~~

A thugged out son,
Wearing thugged out clothes,
Twenty sizes too big,
Waistband held up by his toes.

He is so selfish.
He does not care about anyone.
Disrespecting and abusing women,
Using them for sex and entertaining fun.

He glorifies violent and sexually explicit lyrics,
Blasted so loud like he has a hearing deficit.
Polluting the ears of everyone in his presence.
Puffed up pride is grinning within him.

Money wheeling,
Drug dealing,
Indulging in scandalous sexual acts.

Morally corrupt and bankrupt,
A loss of innocence so hard to get back.

~~~~~~

A daughter out of control,
She wears skimpy clothes.
Her self-respect is long gone…
She lap dances to sexually explicit songs.

Shakin' it, Droppin' it,
Daily selling her soul.
Imitating the girls in music videos
And the ones that swing around poles.

Her tongue spits fire.
Self-destruction boils inside her.
Sucking her teeth and rolling her eyes,
She is a slayer of words of wisdom and guidance.

She only listens to her friends.
She is dominated and ruled by men.

I try to restrict her,
By banning the music and videos from our home.
But I am faced with another obstacle…
I can't be with her everywhere she goes.

~~~~~~

Lord, who is this child stomping all over my heart?

HE was **YOURS** before he was mine.
SHE came from **YOU** before she came from me.

Please humble this child.
Please put an end to this madness.
Please help us Lord.
Please put an end to our sadness.

48

I Believe Lord ...

The One You Need

Matthew 11:28
"Come to me, all you who are weary and burdened, and I will give you rest."

Romans 5:1 & 2
Therefore, since we have been justified through faith, we have peace with God through our Lord Jesus Christ, through whom we have gained access by faith into this grace in which we now stand. And we rejoice in the hope of the glory of God.

When your spirit is low and you feel lost and alone, remember that Jesus is always there to comfort you. Praise, pray, and call on His name. Praise God, giving thanks for all that he has done for you. Pray for Him to help you to stop dwelling on things that you have no control over. Also, pray for comfort, peace, and remedy. Call on His name to rebuke evil thoughts that will keep you trapped in the eye of a storm. We need Jesus to help us make it through every storm in life.

You are in the midst of a storm.
And things are happening...
That you don't quite understand.
Trust that I'll bring you through.

Come; let me hold your hand.

I'm here to tell you...
That I'm the one you need.

Let me show you how,
To cope in this world of troubled times,
Where sin and cold hearts makes love so hard to find.
The blind is leading the blind.

Come walk with me,
I am the love and all the hope you need.

I'm the one your mind is searching for!
I'm the one your heart is aching for!
I'm the one your soul is crying for!
I'm the one you need!

Come to me;
Walk in my light,
It's a safe place to be.
I'll heal your wounds and set your spirit free.

I'm here to tell you,
That I'm the one you need.

I Don't Care What Anyone Says

Psalm 28:7
*The LORD is my strength and my shield; my heart trust in him, and I am
helped. My heart leaps for joy and I will give thanks to him in song.*

Ephesians 6:10 & 11
*Finally, be strong in the Lord and in his mighty power.
Put on the full armor of God so that you can take your stand against the
devil's schemes.*

Struggling with doubt is a very disturbing and dangerous situation for
Christians. Doubt manifests fear, which robs us of confidence and throws us
into depression and a state of hopelessness. When we allow our faith to
become fragile to the comments or actions of unbelievers, we are actually
giving Satan what he wants. The goal of the evil one is to halt our
advancement in our journey towards God's good and perfect plan for our lives.
Do not stumble over the tool of deception called doubt. Always remember
that Jesus is our helper. Success and victory is with everyone who believes in
Him.

I don't care-
What anyone says-
My Jesus **lovvves** me.
Satan **AIN'T** gonna steal **MY** joy away-

The enemy trying so hard
To frustrate me
And ruin **MY** day-

But I call on **MY JESUS,**
There's so much power in His Name!!!

He pours out cooling water on me,
Rinsing the darkness away-
Flowing streams of Holy Spirit ripple just beneath my flesh.
Anointed mercy and grace rescues me from danger,

Gives me victory over another test.
I don't care-
What anyone says-
My Jesus **lovvves** me.
Satan **AIN'T** gonna steal **MY** joy away-

Phew!
I made it through-
Another day-
That old Satan keeps trying to have his way.

Stomping on my spirit,
Jabbing at my mind,
Trying to make me stumble and fall all the time.

I don't care
What anyone says-
As long as I stay with my Sweet Jesus
Everything is gonna be OK...

Spiritual Blackout

We all experience periods of spiritual blackout. It is a time when we are being attacked by Satan and his evil legions. These spirits work hard to interfere with our feeding on God's word. We are mentally crippled when attacked. During this time, praying and reading God's word feels more like a chore instead of a joy. When this happens, immediately tune into a Christian radio station, turn on a Christian TV broadcast, or call a fellow Christian. Instead of reading and praying independently, focus on the Godly words of another Christian. Let their Spirit- filled words penetrate your ears and mind to force the clouds of darkness out of the way.

I'm not sure what to do,
Not sure what to say.
I just can't figure out why I'm feeling this way.

The Lord knows
That I have been trying so hard.
But I am really having a hard time today.

The evil one is distracting me with lies,
Telling me that there is no God,
Asking me, why do you even try?
Here comes those ugly feelings of fear and pity inside.

Wasn't it just yesterday
That I felt like I was on top of the world?
That I could do anything.
I had plenty of faith on reserve.

But today,
I can't even pick up the Word,
I don't even know how to pray.
Feels like I am walking in fog.

Oh, this is really not a good day.

I don't know what to say.
Can't remember what to do.
How do I escape this dark haze?
How do I gain freedom to do what I need to do?

~~~~~~

Thank God that a sister in Christ called and prayed with me.
As I meditated on her words,
I felt freedom unlocking chains,
I sensed darkness being conquered by light.

We are children of God,
And He teaches us that when we come against evil,
It is with prayer that we must fight.

Meant To Be?

Hebrews 6:15
And so after waiting patiently, Abraham received what was promised.

Psalm 130:5
I wait for the LORD, my soul waits and in his word I put my hope.

Some relationships are just not meant to be at all. However, there are some relationships that are meant to be, but the timing may not be right. Recognize when the time has come to let go. Do not be afraid to stand on your own and be single. Learn how to be comfortable with yourself. Stop revisiting heartache by trading in one problem relationship for another. This is not good for you, and for mothers it is especially harmful to children. Ask God to show you who He meant for **YOU** to be. An old saying is, "If you love someone, let them go. If it's meant to be, they will come back to you." Wait for the one who will be capable and willing to work with you as a loving partner. In the meantime, respect yourself, and mothers you must put your children first. Remember the scripture that reads, "What God has put together; no man shall pull apart." You should want that kind of a relationship for your family.

I needed you…
You were not there.

I was always there for you…
You did not care.

I have shown you love…
But you have not been fair.

You planted false hopes,
Pretending to share the dream of you and me,
Finally to be,
Happily ever after…

You said…
That you would marry me!

~~~~~~

Well, I have been waiting for so long,
And you are singing the same old song.
It's finally clear to me,
That this is not meant to be!

So now I must go.
God has been working on me.
He has given me the courage to be single and happy.

I believe that the Lord is faithful,
And that not one of His promises will prove to be empty.
Therefore, I have decided to wait for the one
That He has chosen for me.

Okay Lord ...

Broken For a Reason

Psalm 73:26
My flesh and my heart may fail, but God is the strength of my heart and my portion forever.

Revelation 3:20
Here I am! I stand at the door and knock. If anyone hears my voice and opens the door, I will come in and eat with him, and he with me.

Sometimes there is privilege and purpose in being broken. Privilege is found in being called and chosen by God to participate in His divine plan for humankind. Purpose is experienced by being used by the Lord to accomplish His will. We can never be sure exactly how God is going to use us. We do know that part of our jobs is to bring home our lost sisters and brothers. Therefore, our brokenness allows God to work in our personal relationship with Him, but it also moves us to witness to others. However, a blessing always accompanies brokenness if we obey God's commands for our lives and share His message of hope with lost souls.

I went to a place-
That I never thought I would go.
My spirit would go very high,
But then it would drop unbearably low.

Heart beating so fast,
Thought it would fail me for sure,
Plunged into an emotional crisis,
I desperately needed a cure.

I went to a place
That I never thought I would go.
Hospitalized with others,
Feeling lost and alone.

Some suffered with mental illness,
Drugs and alcohol gripped some souls.
But this was a purpose-filled journey;
I had to share a message of hope.

As I spoke about Jesus Christ,
Many were eager to know the Word.
The presence of the Lord filled the air;
God's call is what they heard

I went to a place
That I never thought I would go,
I was sent by the Lord,
To touch other troubled souls.

I shared the gospel of Jesus Christ,
How He made the ultimate sacrifice,
So that we may be forgiven for our sins,
So that we may inherit eternal life.

So You Want To Serve The Lord?

1 Peter 4:12 & 13
Dear friends, do not be surprised at the painful trial you are suffering as though something strange were happening to you. But rejoice that you participate in the sufferings of Christ, so that you may be overjoyed when his glory is revealed.

Romans 12:1
Therefore, I urge you, brothers, in view of God's mercy, to offer your bodies as living sacrifices, holy and pleasing to God - this is your spiritual act of worship.

Life as a Christian can be very enjoyable and rewarding, yet difficult at the same time. There are many tests and obstacles we face daily. We have tests of faith in this dying world, tests of will in this immoral world, and tests of goodness and kindness in this hardened world. However, we can overcome all difficulties and maintain our worthiness to serve with continued growth in all things instructed by our Lord and Savior Jesus Christ.

So you want to serve the Lord?
Well tell me,
What can you afford?

What will it cost you to lose some family and friends?
Will it break your heart to feel lonely within?

What if your house was no longer your home?
Would a downgrade and what others may think put an aching in your bones?

How will you avoid sexual immorality?
Will your spirit die from lack of sinful activity?

What if someone slanders your character and your name?
Will you remain humble and meek?
Or will you seek revenge because turning a cheek
Burns like hot coals, causing your ego too much pain.

I tell you now,
These are some tests and trials that you may have to endure,
But keeping faith in Jesus Christ will make your calling and election secure.

Therefore: To **Faith,** add **Goodness**

To goodness, **Knowledge**

To knowledge, **Self Control**

To self control, **Perseverance**

To perseverance, **Godliness**

To godliness, **Brotherly Kindness**

To brotherly kindness, **Love**

Do these things, and your rewards will be far greater than what you can afford.

When They Ask Who I Am!!

Exodus 3:14
God said to Moses, "I AM WHO I AM. This is what you are to say to the Israelites: 'I AM has sent me to you.'"

Ephesians 5:6
Let no one deceive you with empty words, for because of such things God's wrath comes on those who are disobedient.

God is Father and Master of all creation. He has complete sovereignty. There is nothing or anything that can or will be without God's approval and grace. One of the names of God in the Old Testament, "I AM," indicates that God is involved in the lives of mankind. God makes promises, and then he causes things to happen to fulfill those promises. Jesus called himself "I AM" in the New Testament to indicate that he is the bread of life and is God in the flesh.

You are Wonderful!
You are Magnificent!
You are So Great!
You are All Mighty!

But none of these words seem to completely
Personify your awesomeness.

So when asked who you are,
What do I say?

In the scriptures you said:
I AM WHO I AM!!

Some may ask… Am who?

My dear child…
That is the very point at hand,
I AM too much for any human to understand.

I AM the source of all things!
I AM Creator of everything!
I speak! And things come to be!

That's why---
I AM WHO I AM!!

Tell them to trust and obey,
And that it is **<u>NOT</u>** wise to
Go against what I say.

And when they ask,
"Go against what *who* says???"

Tell them that…
MY
NAME
IS

I AM!!!

<u>*Not Me, But He*</u>

1 Peter 4:10 & 11
Each one should use whatever gift he has received to serve others, faithfully administering God's grace in its various forms. If anyone speaks, he should do it as one speaking the very words of God...

Ephesians 4:11& 12
It was he who gave some to be apostles, some to be prophets, some to be evangelist, and some to be pastors and teachers, to prepare God's people for works of service,

Every child of God is blessed with a spiritual gift from God; therefore, we will be great at what God ordains us to do. However, we must never think of ourselves as greater than any other member of our Christian family. We must keep in mind that it is only by God's grace that we can do what we do. Nothing is of our own ability, strength, or knowledge. We must always be meek and humble when sharing our gift with others. We cannot allow conceit or arrogance to enter our lives. No Glory whatsoever belongs to man. In the Old Testament, God left us a reminder: Moses was not allowed to enter the Promise Land because he took credit for bringing water from the rock. How much greater are we than Moses? Not at all!!!

Please!!! Do not give unjustified credit to me

Know that it is…
Not me,
But He.

Know that He is using me.

Know that I am just a vessel,
An artery,
A small vein,
Delivering a message for He.

Not for Me, But He.
66

Yes, I am anointed and ordained.
But nothing evil flees from my name.
So please don't give the credit to me
Because no matter how good my performance will be,
It's only by God's grace which inspires me.

Therefore, I welcome the applaud,
But please make no mistake about who gets the Glory.

It's **Not** Me-
But He-

Thank You Lord!!!

Thank You for Hearing My Cry

Isaiah 64:8
O, LORD, you are our Father. We are the clay, you are the potter; we are all the work of your hand.

Psalm 40:1
I wait patiently for the LORD, he turned to me and heard my cry.

If life's struggles and disappointments have weighed you down, call on the Lord. If life feels empty and hopeless, draw close to God. This will be the most important and fulfilling relationship that you will ever establish. Promises that men make and break can be fulfilled by God. God is a God of love. He will never hurt or disappoint you. So, let go of those burdens. Surrender to God's will. Allow Him to lead you on the journey that He has planned for you. And when you feel like you have been waiting for so long for a blessing, remember this: waiting on God does not yield disappointment; waiting on God can only yield perfection. God is an awesome God and His perfect plan is worth waiting for.

Lord, please hear me…

My emotions are all mixed up,
I'm not sure who really cares.
Can anyone be trusted?
It's really lonely 'round here.

Lord, I can't cope anymore,
I'm mentally lost and unclear,
I can't find comfort in anything,
I'm confined by depression and despair.

Where do I find peace?
Will happiness step in?
In this crazy mixed up world,
That is feasting on sin?

70

I've been in this space too long,
With emptiness as natural as the wind,
Running on low voltage energy,
All joy has expired within.

Outdone by disappointments,
And crippled by fear,
Another dream fades away
With every lost tear.

I want to run away and hide;
I need to escape from here to anywhere.
Desperate for freedom
From these weights I bear.

I have to reach the destiny
That You prescribed for me,
Just need to know how to get there.
I need to learn who you want me to be.

Please Lord, fill me with courage
And strengthen my faith.
Today I surrender my soul to you;
For a long time this was a hard choice to make.

Transform and mold me,
Into whom you want me to be.
Guide me on this journey
To where fulfillment runs free.

And Lord, I do have one dream left,
Despite many lost tears.
It is the sum of all the rest.

And in it-
Love, peace, and security
Are waiting-
For me!

All adorned in tears of joy,
The tears that could not flow free.
Ready to do as you told them,
All anxious to greet and embrace me!

To make my life complete!
And to lift my spirit up high!
All because **YOU** love me.

Thank you Lord,
For hearing my cry!!!

Thank You Lord for Loving Me

Psalm 40:2
He lifted me out of the slimy pit, out of the mud and mire; he set my feet on a rock and gave me a firm place to stand.

1John 1:5 & 7
This is the message we have heard from him and declare to you: God is light; in him there is no darkness at all. If we claim to have fellowship with him yet walk in the darkness, we lie and do not live by the truth. But if we walk in light, as he is in the light, we have fellowship with one another, and the blood of Jesus, his Son, purifies us from all sin.

Every day we should thank God for what he has done for us. Thank him for loving us and having mercy on our imperfect souls. Keep in mind that continuous praise in conjunction with reading and meditating on God's Word are weapons against the evil one. Also, be reminded that true joy and happiness cannot be found in worldly things. Chasing after and obtaining all the worldly things possible for our own pleasure will still inevitably leave us feeling void and empty if God is not first in our lives. Therefore, pursue God and immerse yourself in the eternal joy that accompanies a close relationship with Him. Cling to the salvation that He so mercifully offers to us. These are things of substance, full of value and meaning.

Without you, where would I be?
Without you, how could I see?

Without you, life was so empty.
Thank You Lord for loving me.

I can't bear to think of life without you.
You make me happy; your love is true.

Thank you for bringing me out of darkness.
Thank you for shining your light on me.
Thank you for renewing my mind.
Thank you Lord for forgiving me.

I don't have the strength to face this world without you.
You are my rock;
You see me through all situations no matter how big or small.
Your love and grace makes me walk tall.

Thank you for cleansing me.
Thank you for showing me the vanity
Of pursuing knowledge, power, and wealth.

Thank you for healing me.
Thank you for giving me anointed sanity.
Thank You Lord for loving me.

What a joy it is now that I am learning how
To work out my salvation with trembling and fear.

Eternal salvation promised and so real
Because of You who works in me to act and do
According to Your good and perfect will.

Thank You Lord for loving me.

A Poetic Walk of Faith

Address a variety of life issues and situations. Every individual has relationships and situations unique to their own set of life circumstances. However, regardless who the woman is or what her life situations are, the journey towards Godly destiny must begin with a healing process. The first step is to let go of hurts and pains of the past. Confess all of your sins to God, and ask Him for forgiveness. Then, forgive yourself. Finally, you must forgive everyone who has ever done wrong to you. The best way to accomplish this is by living in today, not yesterday or tomorrow. Take one day at a time, walking with Jesus as your guide. Remember that every step in the right direction, regardless of how small the step, is a step to be proud of.

When you walk with God, He will reveal the power, strength, courage, and determination hidden inside of you. Start by acknowledging the issues in your life that are preventing you from growing as a person. Change the things that you have the power to change. Remove negative people and negative situations from your life. Be confident and know that you are a beautiful, wonderful child of God.

This journey will be a purpose filled journey. There will be peaks and valleys. There will be tests and trials that will have to be overcome, but always remember that all things (good and bad) work together for the good of those who love the Lord. Along the way, valuable life lessons will be learned to strengthen faith. My goal is for this book to serve as a spiritual reference for specific issues that you may face during your journey. You can find a poem related to an issue, and seek spiritual guidance through the Word of God. You should not stop with the scriptures referenced in the poem; instead, make them a starting point. Dig into the Word of God. Search, search, and search. You will find your search to be a good way to study the Bible, which will prove to be a life changing experience.

ABOUT THE AUTHOR

Alesia W. Green is the mother of three boys and she has faced many trials and challenges in life from juggling work, home, and relationships. After many years of perservering through it all, she found that she was running out of energy and having trouble coping with new issues. The stresses and pressures of life were escalating out of control. Insanity was knocking at her door and panic was racing around her like a mad-man set free. The fragile walls of her life were crumbling down around her. She was outdone, broken, and ready to end it all. But instead Alesia surrendered to the will of God. He gave her new hope for life and the future.

CPSIA information can be obtained
at www.ICGtesting.com
Printed in the USA
BVHW031127060321
601818BV00019B/305